I0823263

INTO THE UNKNOWN

GHOSTS AND SPIRITS

Kevin Cunningham

Mitchell Lane PUBLISHERS

Mitchell Lane
PUBLISHERS

mitchelllanepub.com

2001 SW 31st Avenue
Hallandale, FL 33009

First Edition, 2026.
Author: Kevin Cunningham
Designer: Ed Morgan
Editor: Morgan Brody

Series: Into the Unknown
Title: Ghosts and Spirits

Library bound ISBN: 979-8-89260-736-0
eBook ISBN: 979-8-89260-743-8

Photo credits: cover, 2, 3, 5, 9, 13, 19, 21, 23, 32 freepik.com; p. 4, 11, 15, 25 Shutterstock; p. 7 Alamy; p. 17, 27 wikimedia

CONTENTS

CHAPTER ONE

LA LLARONA

Jenara Cano lived in Xaibe Village, Belize. People had talked about La Llorona her whole life.

"Right before someone dies La Llorona comes and it gives you chills and makes you afraid," Cano told Channel 5 Belize. "Last month a lady in front of us died and I heard La Llorona."

La Llorona is an important **legend**. Spanish-speakers in Mexico, parts of Latin America, and the US tell stories about the ghost.

CHAPTER ONE

La Llorona's name means *weeping woman*. The spirit shrieks and cries. She committed evil acts. She must haunt the earth. In other versions, La Llorona searches for her children. Or she seeks revenge on men. These legends say she was a woman named Maria. A man broke her heart.

La Llorona often appears near water. Modern versions also place her along roads or in cities. La Llorona may have a skeleton's face or no face at all. It depends on the story.

Parents sometimes use La Llorona to scare kids into behaving. Esperanza Sernas told the American Folklife Center: "I remember that they used to say that if you don't go to school, or if you don't do this or that, La Llorona will appear to you and carry you off."

Ghosts haunt people and places around the world. Many have a tale that explains why they exist. Others turn up for no reason. People everywhere love ghost stories.

FAST FACT

Pieces of the La Llorona legend go back centuries. The Aztec people of Central Mexico told stories of a weeping woman. The Aztec goddess Cihuacoatl also became part of the La Llorona legend.

CHAPTER TWO

HAUNTED WORLD

Ghosts may roam the place where they suffered. Burnt Woman haunts an area in New South Wales, Australia. The **indigenous** Bandjaland people say that long ago a woman died in a fire. She came back as a spirit. Burnt Woman often appears to visitors. She chooses to frighten men in particular.

CHAPTER TWO

In many places, ghosts want revenge. The onryō in Japan often suffered a wrong while alive. The spirit returns to get even. The powerful onryō may unleash illness or an earthquake. People calm the ghost by righting the wrong.

Ghosts may predict death. Irish tradition tells of the banshee. A banshee wails, or keens, to warn that someone will soon die. Many Irish families have their own banshee.

Certain ghosts just scare people. In Nigeria, Madame Koi Koi walks around schools and places where students live. The ghost wears red shoes. People might stay away from a building for days after Madame Koi Koi visits.

FAST FACT

Not all ghosts appear as figures of people. Balls of light called ghost orbs show up in photos and videos. Non-believers say light shining on dust or water drops creates orbs.

CHAPTER TWO

Finally, some ghosts want to help. There was a popular **urban legend** in San Antonio, Texas. Cars sometimes stalled while going over haunted railroad tracks. Ghost children appeared and pushed the car to safety.

Ghosts become part of history. Ghosts let people believe in otherworldly things. But some people go beyond telling stories. They search for evidence that ghosts really exist.

FAST FACT

The phantom hitchhiker is a popular urban legend. Resurrection Mary haunts the road outside a cemetery in Illinois. A driver gives a woman a ride. She vanishes before the car passes the cemetery. A phantom hitchhiker outside Uniondale, South Africa, appears (and disappears) in almost the same way. A ghostly couple flags down drivers on a forest road in India.

CHAPTER THREE

GHOST HUNTING

The German word **poltergeist** means "noisy spirit." Poltergeists slam doors and pound walls. Plates fly across the kitchen. Lamps fall down. The Enfield poltergeist moved around furniture.

Ghost-hunters investigate **paranormal** events. Hauntings like poltergeists get their attention.

CHAPTER THREE

Borley Rectory was a famous British haunted house. People reported strange happenings for years. Bells rang for no reason. Windows shattered. The ghost of a nun appeared. Doors locked people into rooms.

Paranormal investigator Harry Price visited the house in 1929. The ghosts put on a show. He called the visit, "Sixteen hours of thrills." Price later declared Borley Rectory "the most haunted house in England."

FAST FACT

A spirit haunted the Bell family from 1817 to 1821. It happened in Tennessee. People heard knocking sounds and chains pulled across the floor. A weird animal appeared. The spirit pinched, pulled hair, and spoke. People referred to the ghost as the Bell Witch.

CHAPTER THREE

Hans Holzer called a ghost "a fellow human being in trouble." Holzer taught at the New York Institute of Technology. Many ghosts, he believed, were just lost and confused. Holzer investigated a haunted house in Amityville, New York. He wrote several books about it.

Today's ghost hunters may star in an online video or TV show. Others chase spirits for fun.

Many investigators use instruments to find evidence. Cameras snap glowing shapes. Heat sensing gadgets detect cold spots left by spirits. Spirit boxes capture ghostly voices in radio static. There are apps that turn a smartphone into a spirit box.

Non-believers view ghosts as make-believe. Some seek to **debunk** ghost stories. Many of them have succeeded.

FAST FACT

Guests across the US pay money for paranormal tours of places like mansions and old hospitals. Kevin Armbrust of the Acadia Ranch Museum told Bloomberg.com, “We don’t say that ghosts actually exist, but we don’t say they don’t either.”

CHAPTER FOUR

BEHIND THE MYSTERY

Skeptics investigate ghostly events. Evidence explains most hauntings.

Take the child ghosts in San Antonio. The haunting began after a train hit a school bus. But that accident happened in another city. An incline helped cars roll off the tracks, not ghosts.

Harry Price knew magic tricks. His magic probably caused the poltergeist events. The poltergeist acted up when he visited. The trouble ended when he left. A team of investigators checked Price's stories. Their report debunked everything.

CHAPTER FOUR

Researchers noted problems with the haunted house in Amityville, New York. For example, others lived in the house without trouble from spirits. A man admitted the truth. He dreamed up the story. The couple that reported the haunting helped him.

Many people honestly believe they encountered a ghost. Chris French studied why humans believe in the paranormal. He thought the **power of suggestion** may affect ghost hunters.

"If you're shown around an old building and somebody says it's haunted," French said to Bbc.com, "you'll notice every little creak and change in temperature in a way you wouldn't have done otherwise."

The power of suggestion can be powerful. A person really wants ghosts to exist. They find reasons to believe. But their hopes can make it easier for a dishonest person to trick them.

FAST FACT

Vic Tandy worked in his laboratory. He felt a chill. He saw a gray ghost, The next day Tandy returned. He brought a sword he used in fencing. The tip vibrated. Tandy investigated. A new fan system gave off a hum too low for humans to hear. The sound caused Tandy's eyes to vibrate. He "saw" a ghost. Low sounds also affected his body. That's why he felt a chill.

CHAPTER FIVE

FAMOUS FAKE PHANTOMS

Harry Price played a **hoax**. But fake phantoms go back centuries.

In 1762, Scratching Fanny excited all of London. The ghost made knocking and scratching noises. Everyone wanted to see for themselves. The home's owner Richard Parsons charged money to get in. Scratching Fanny turned out to be Parsons's eleven-year-old daughter. Parsons went to prison.

CHAPTER FIVE

The Fox sisters' hoax had an even bigger effect. Maggie, aged 14, and Kate, aged 11, claimed to be **mediums**. They asked spirits questions. The spirits knocked out answers on walls or floors. Maggie and Kate toured with a show. They demonstrated their skill.

Their claims helped launch a movement. Spiritualism became popular. Mediums appeared all over the US.

Maggie confessed 40 years later. She had faked her powers from the start. "We used to tie an apple on a string and move the string up and down, causing the apple to bump on the floor," she said. The girls also made knocking noises by cracking their knuckles and joints.

The power of suggestion played a part, too. As Maggie said, "A great many people when they hear the rapping imagine at once that the spirits are touching them. Of course that was pure imagination."

Believers and skeptics search for evidence of ghosts. So far, the evidence says that ghosts only haunt our imaginations. But ghost stories remain as popular as ever.

FAST FACT

William H. Mumler began to snap pictures of ghosts in 1861. The image of a customer's loved one appeared in the customer's portrait. Mumler used his knowledge of photography to pull off the trick. Eight years later, Mumler stood trial for using false claims to take people's money.

TIMELINE

1500 BCE	The earliest known image of a ghost is possibly pressed onto a clay tablet
1762	The ghost Scratching Fanny becomes a celebrity in London
1817–1821	A spirit haunts the Bell family in Tennessee
1848	Maggie and Kate Fox first trick people by creating knocking sounds
1861	William H. Mumler takes his first "spirit photograph"
1929	Harry Price makes his first visit to the Borley Rectory
1939	Jerry Palus reports one of the earliest sightings of Resurrection Mary
2021	A YouGov survey finds 41% of Americans believe in ghosts

GLOSSARY

debunk (DEE-bunk)
Disprove a false claim

hoax (HOKS)
A fake or trick used to deceive others

indigenous (in-DIH-je-nus)
The original inhabitants of a region

legend (LEH-jend)
An unproven story that may be treated as a fact

medium (MEE-dee-um)
A person who claims to contact the spirits of dead people

paranormal (PAH-reh-NOR-mal)
Beyond scientific understanding

poltergeist (POL-ter-gyst)
A ghost or spirit that causes loud noises and moves objects

power of suggestion (POW-er ov se-JES-chen)
The ability of an idea or belief to affect how a person thinks or feels

skeptic (SKEP-tik)
A person who doubts or questions an idea

urban legend (UHR-ban LEJ-uhnd)
A scary story without proof that is told as if it were true

FACT CHECK

1. **What do we call a kind of noisy ghost known for pounding walls and making other sounds?**

   A. Madame Koi Koi
   B. Poltergeist
   C. Ghoul
   D. Maggie Fox

2. **Why does the ghostly onryō haunt the world of the living?**

   A. To warn trespassers away from cemeteries
   B. To protect children
   C. To predict the future
   D. To take revenge

3. **People tell many La Llorona tales, but most stories agree the ghost makes which sound?**

   A. A loud weeping
   B. Heavy footsteps
   C. A howl like a coyote
   D. Flapping bird wings

4. **The case of the Borley Rectory ghost turned out which way?**

   A. As the real ghost of someone who died in the house
   B. As raccoons living behind the walls
   C. As a hoax created by Harry Price and others
   D. As pieces of the house falling down

Answers: B, D, A, C

FIND OUT MORE

IN PRINT

Fitzpatrick, Insha. *Chilling with Ghosts: A Totally Factual Field Guide to the Supernatural*. Philadelphia: Quirk Books, 2023.

Leaf, Christina. *Ghosts in Africa*. Minnetonka, MN: Bellwether Media, 2021.

Peterson, Megan Cooley. *The Bell Witch: An American Ghost Story*. North Mankato, MN: Capstone, 2019.

ON THE INTERNET

BBC Earth Science. "The Science of Ghosts." Via YouTube. Video. Undated.
www.youtube.com/watch?v=FuFZf89Rp-A

Public Broadcasting System. "The Legend of La Llorona." Pbs.org. July 3, 2019. Video.
www.pbs.org/video/the-legend-of-la-llorona-asl-rglm7g

PBS Voices. "These Children Could Talk to Dead People, but It Was a Prank." Via YouTube. October 20, 2022. Video.

INDEX

About the Author

Kevin Cunningham has written over 120 books on history, medicine, careers, and climate change. He lives near Chicago, Illinois. A ghost supposedly lived in a sawmill near his cousin's house.